JAZZ GUITAR CHORD MELODY SOLOS

Irving Berlin

27 Chord Melody Arrangements in
Standard Notation & Tablature

Arrangements by Gabriel Davila and Bill LaFleur

ISBN 978-1-4234-3701-7

Blue Skies™ is a trademark of the Estate of Irving Berlin

Irving Berlin logo and Irving Berlin Music Company are registered
trademarks of the Estate of Irving Berlin

Irving Berlin Music Company®

www.irvingberlin.com

EXCLUSIVELY DISTRIBUTED BY

HAL•LEONARD®
CORPORATION

7777 W. BLUEMOUND RD. P.O. BOX 13819 MILWAUKEE, WI 53213

Visit Hal Leonard Online at www.halleonard.com

Irving Berlin

Alexander's Ragtime Band

from ALEXANDER'S RAGTIME BAND
Words and Music by Irving Berlin

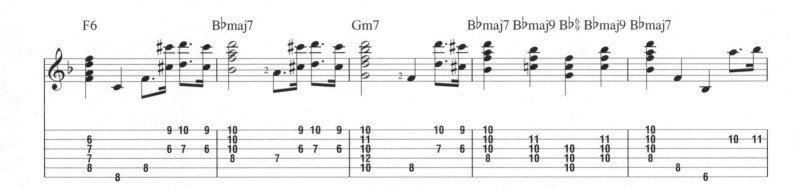

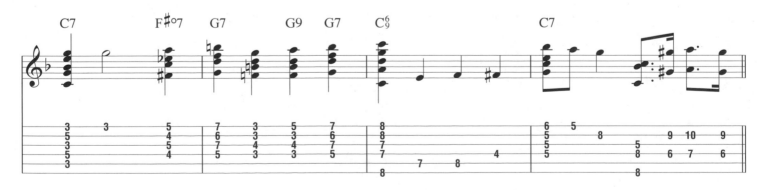

B

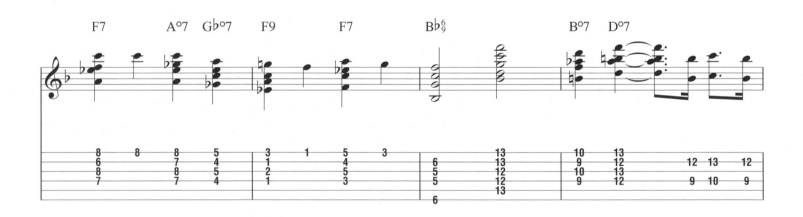

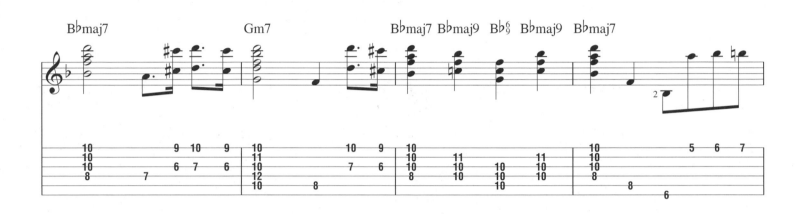

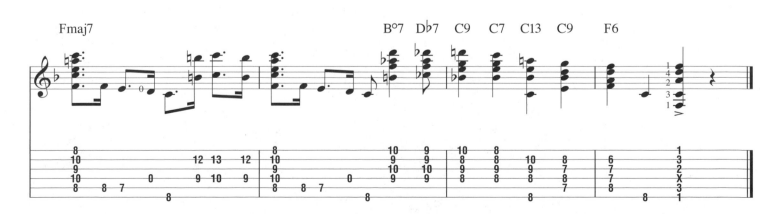

All Alone

Words and Music by Irving Berlin

Moderately

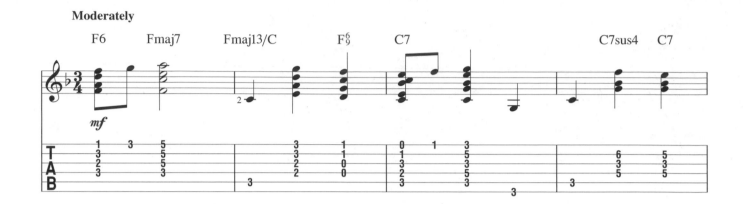

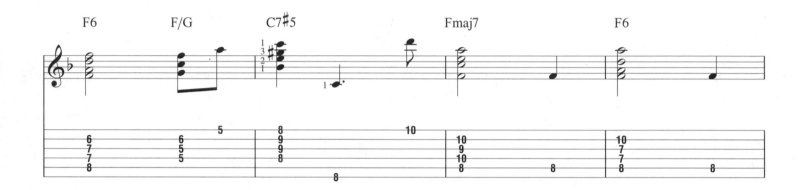

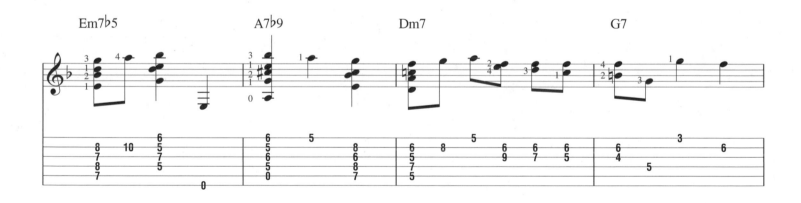

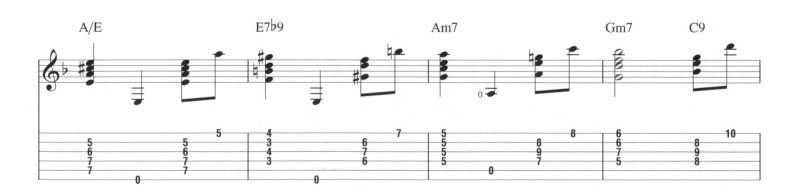

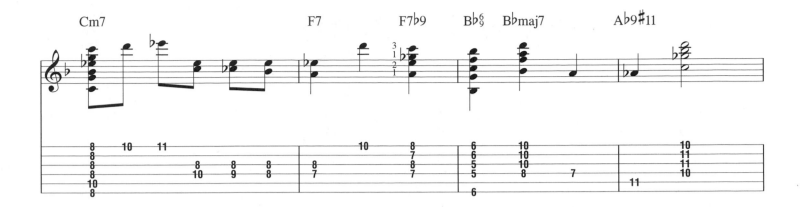

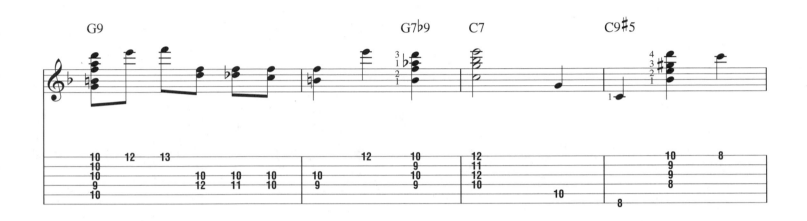

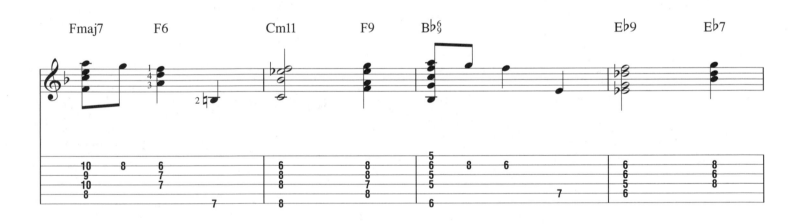

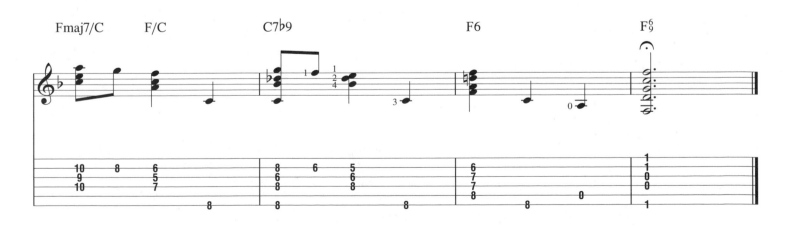

All by Myself

Words and Music by Irving Berlin

A

Moderately

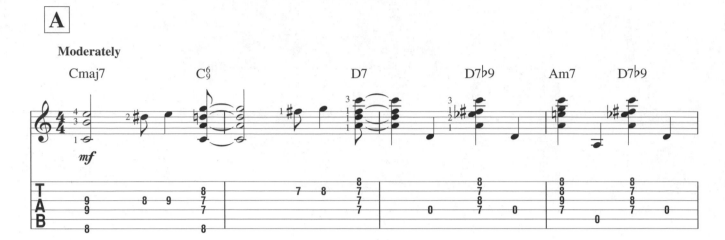

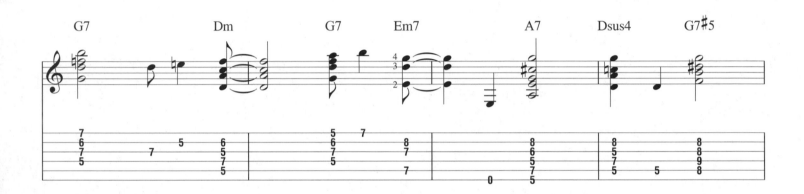

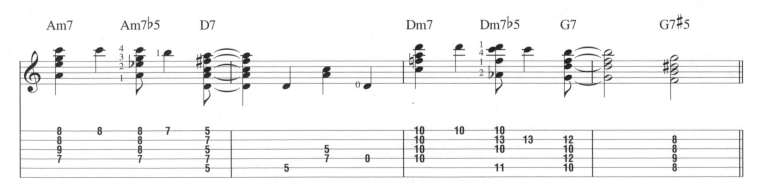

B

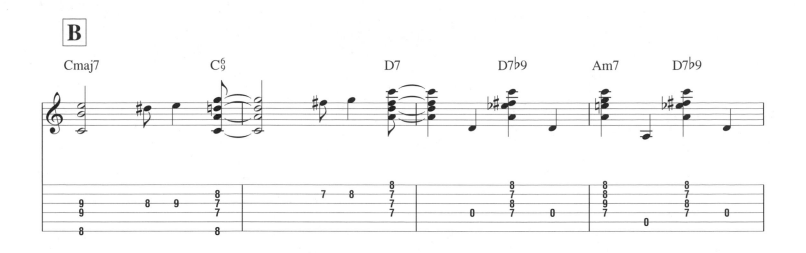

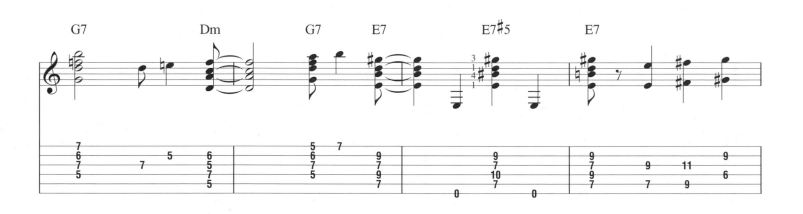

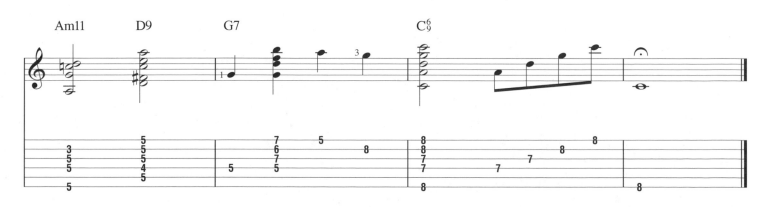

Always

Words and Music by Irving Berlin

A

Moderately slow

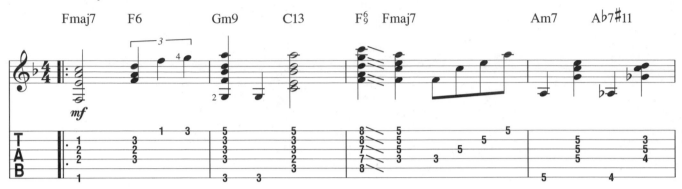

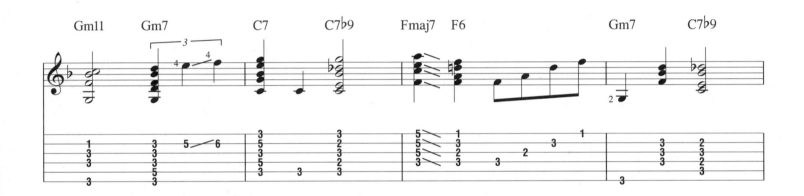

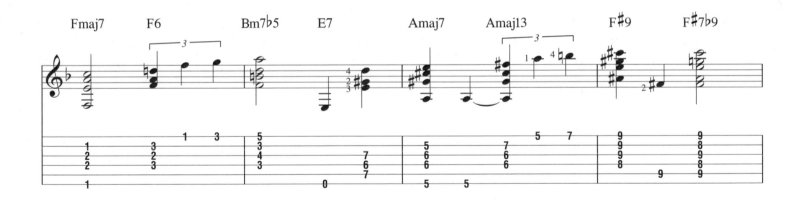

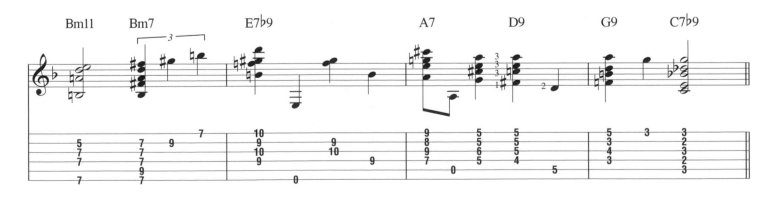

B

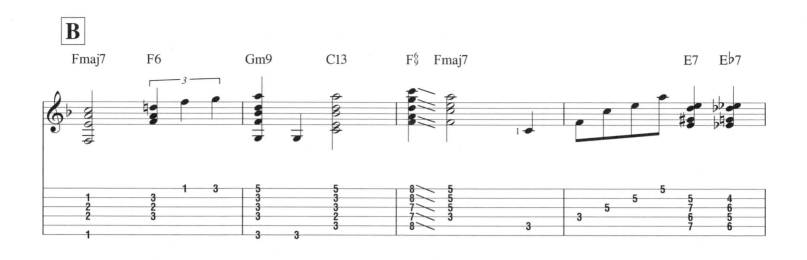

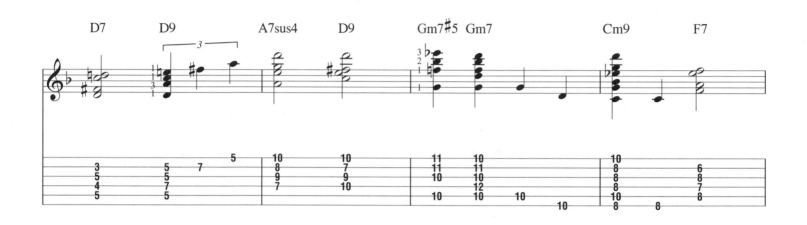

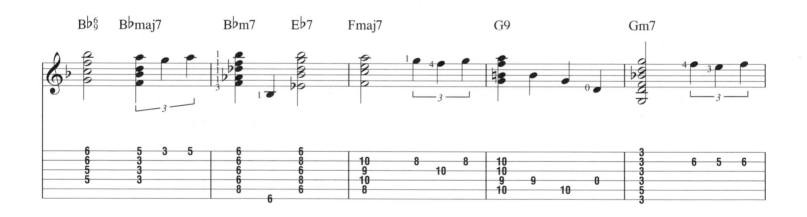

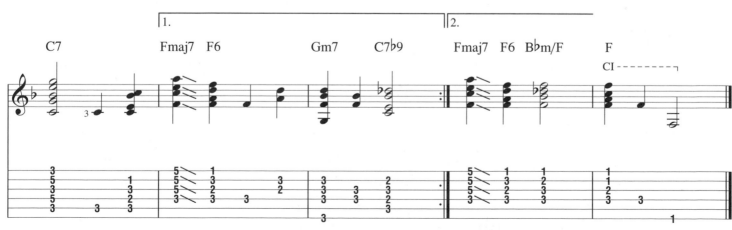

Change Partners

from the RKO Radio Motion Picture CAREFREE
Words and Music by Irving Berlin

B

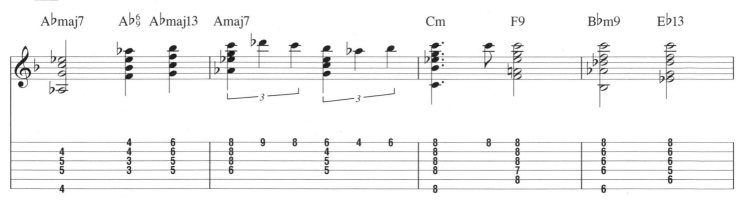

D.C. al Coda

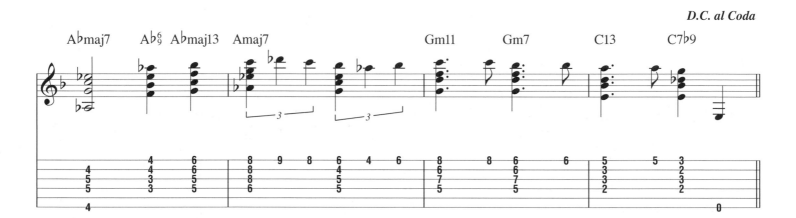

Coda

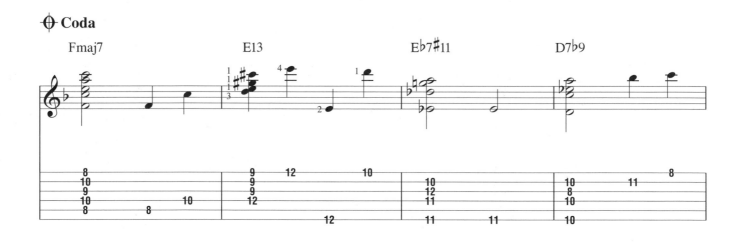

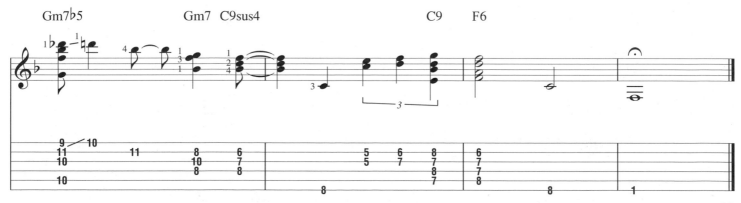

Blue Skies

from BETSY

Words and Music by Irving Berlin

Cheek to Cheek

from the RKO Radio Motion Picture TOP HAT
Words and Music by Irving Berlin

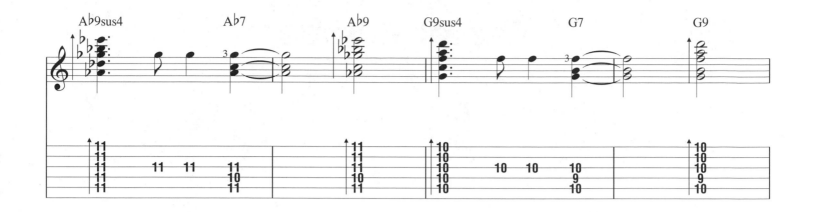

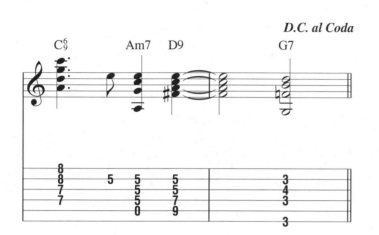

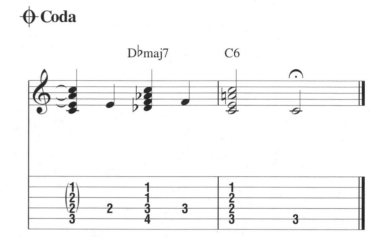

Easter Parade

from AS THOUSANDS CHEER
Words and Music by Irving Berlin

A

Moderately

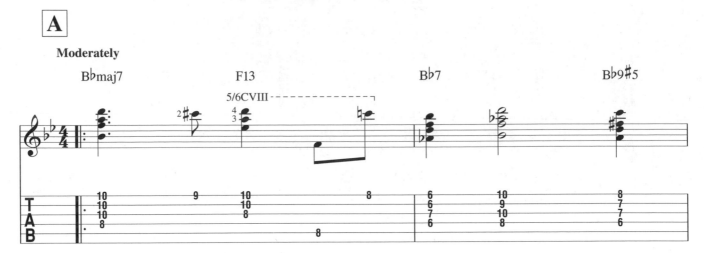

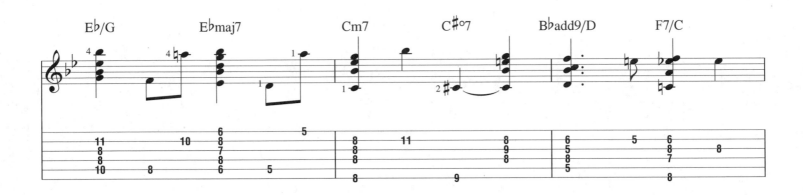

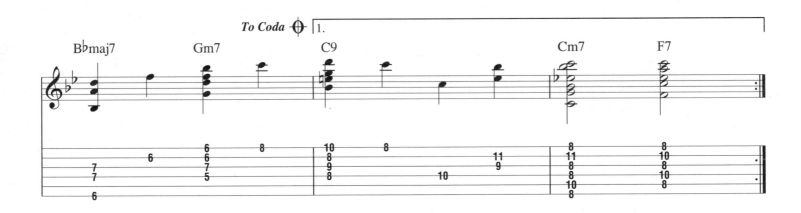

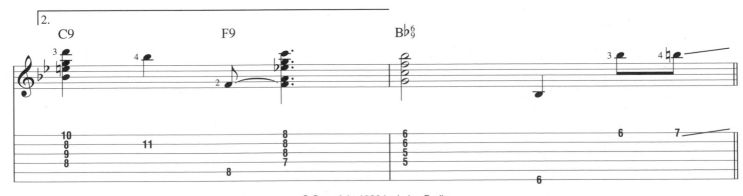

B

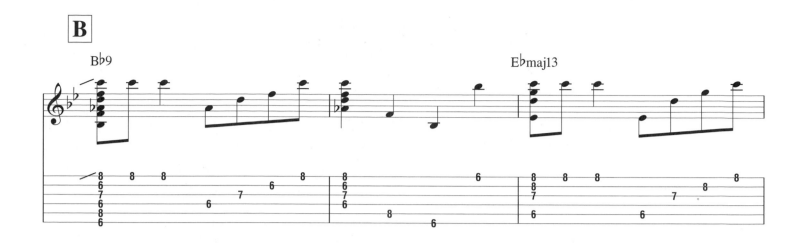

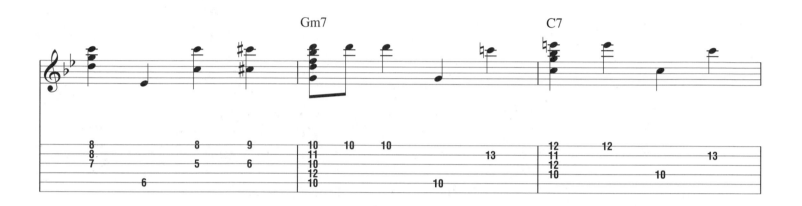

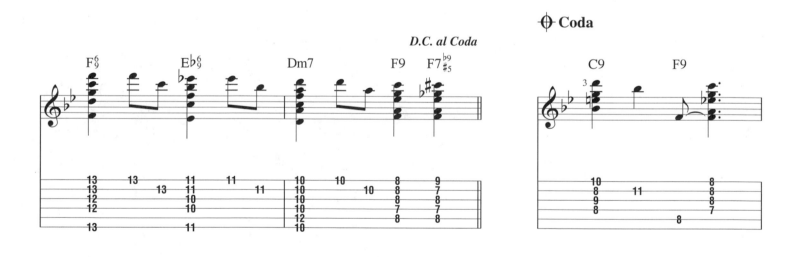

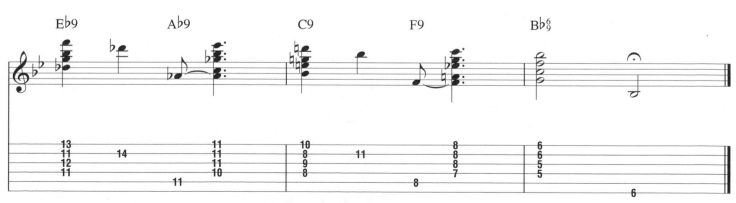

19

Happy Holiday

from the Motion Picture Irving Berlin's HOLIDAY INN
Words and Music by Irving Berlin

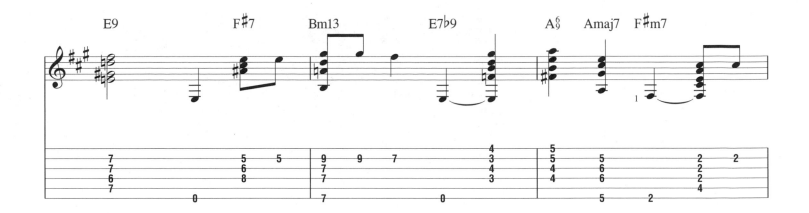

Heat Wave

from the Stage Production AS THOUSANDS CHEER
from the Motion Picture ALEXANDER'S RAGTIME BAND
from THERE'S NO BUSINESS LIKE SHOW BUSINESS
Words and Music by Irving Berlin

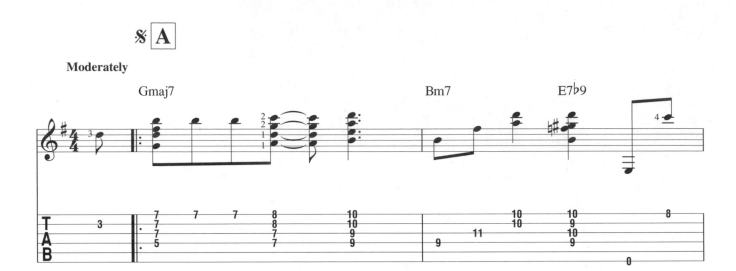

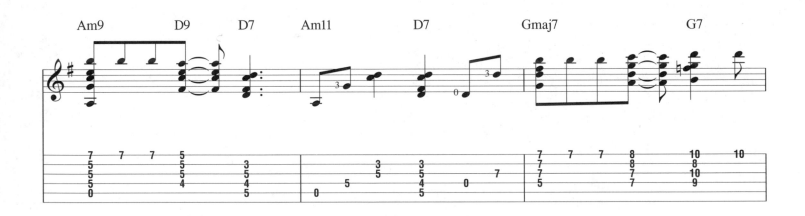

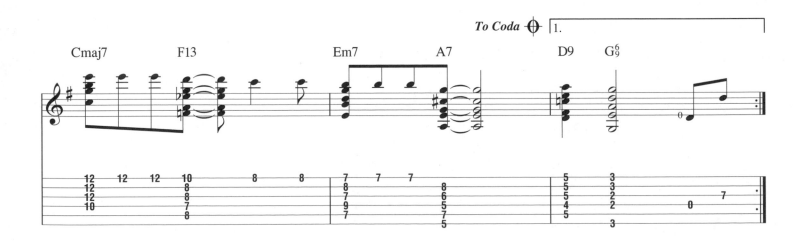

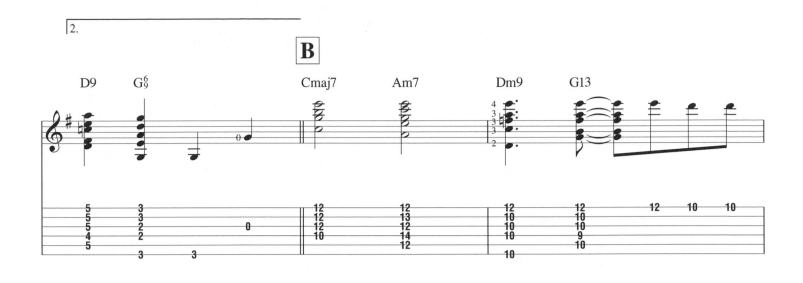

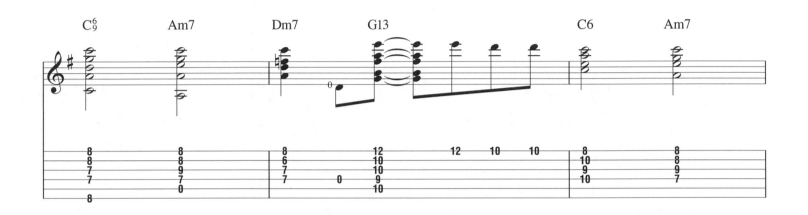

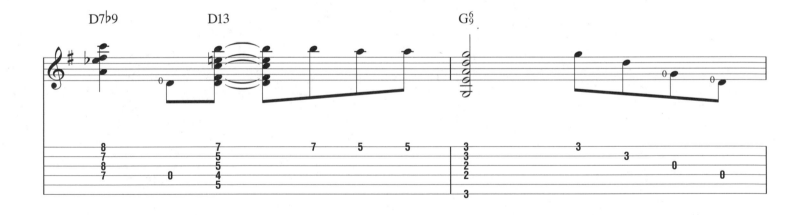

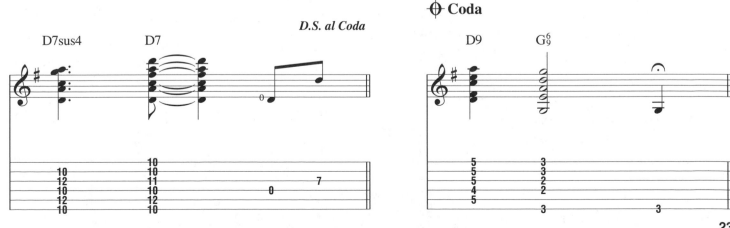

23

How Deep Is the Ocean

(How High Is the Sky)

Words and Music by Irving Berlin

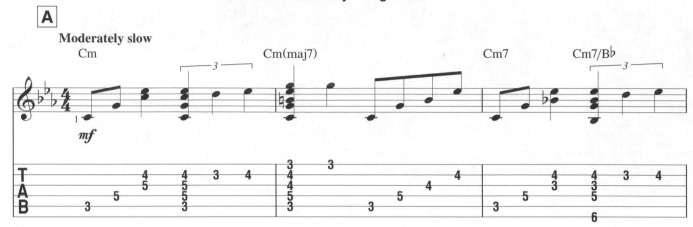

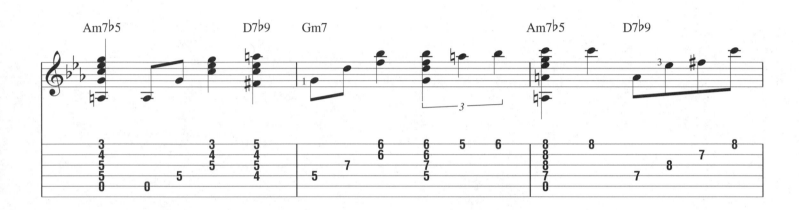

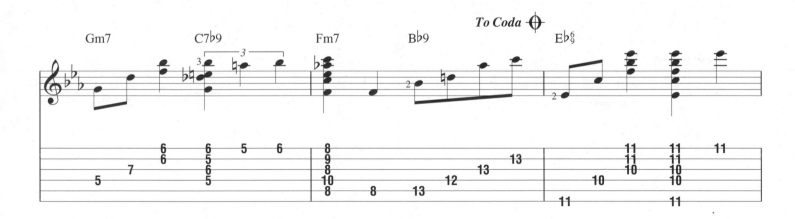

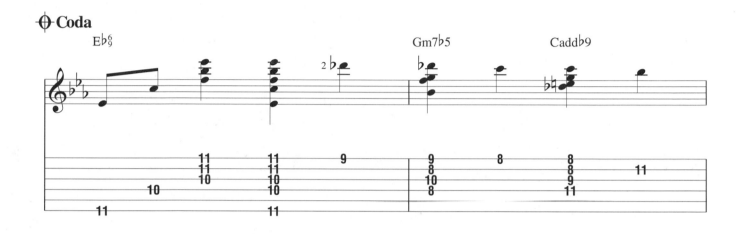

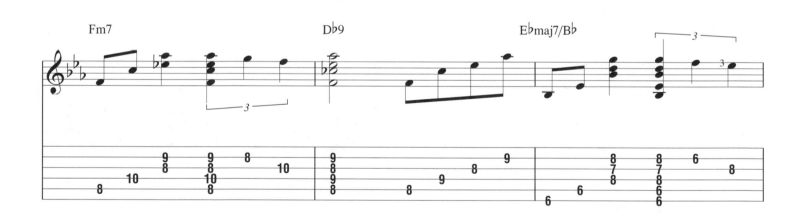

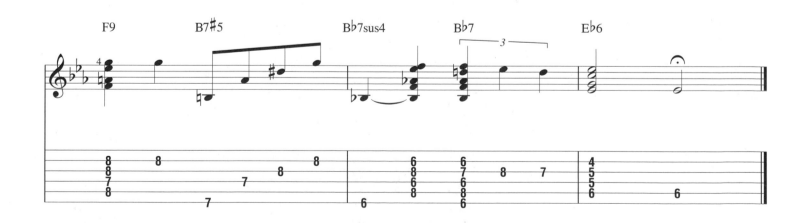

I'm Putting All My Eggs in One Basket

from the Motion Picture FOLLOW THE FLEET
Words and Music by Irving Berlin

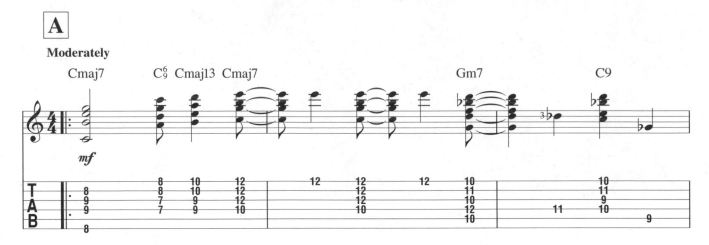

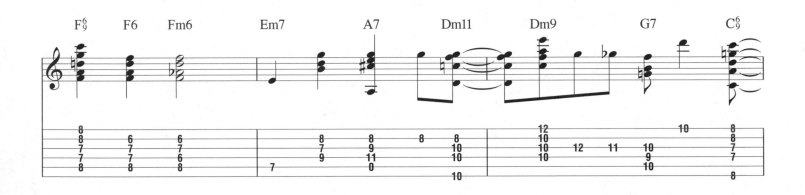

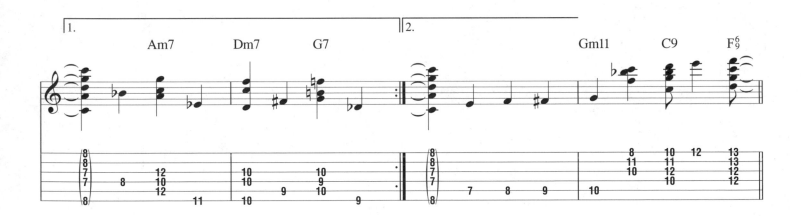

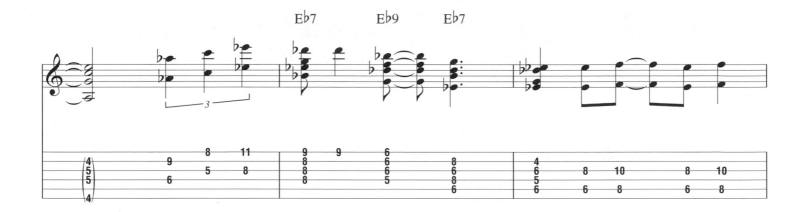

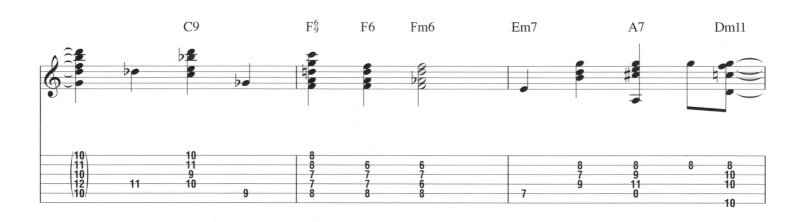

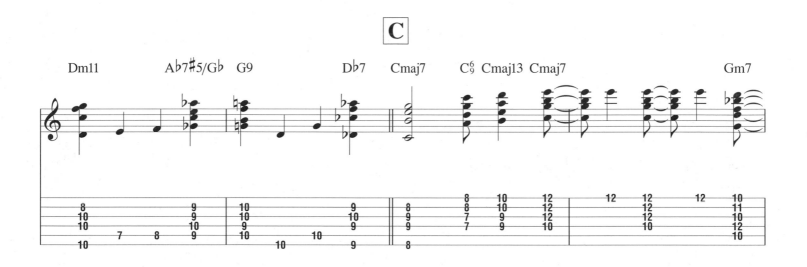

I've Got My Love to Keep Me Warm

from the 20th Century Fox Motion Picture ON THE AVENUE
Words and Music by Irving Berlin

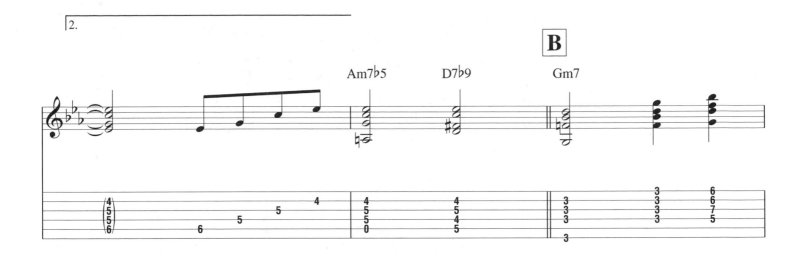

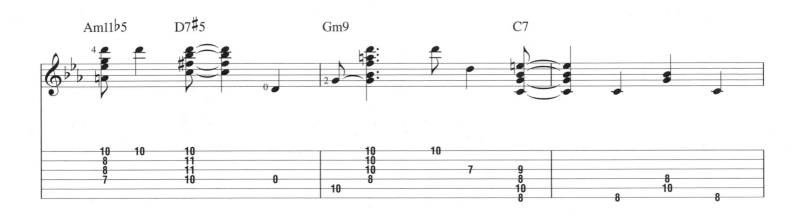

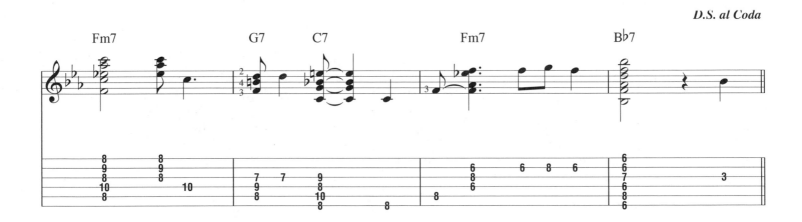

D.S. al Coda

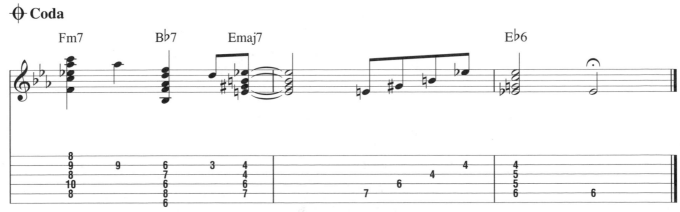

Isn't This a Lovely Day
(To Be Caught in the Rain?)

from the RKO Radio Motion Picture TOP HAT
Words and Music by Irving Berlin

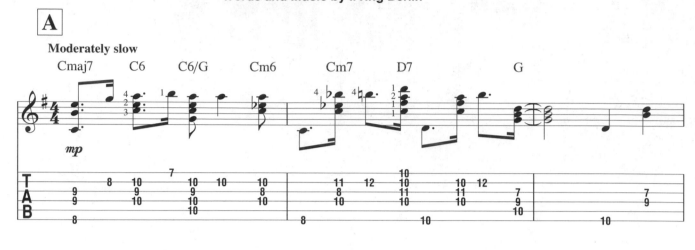

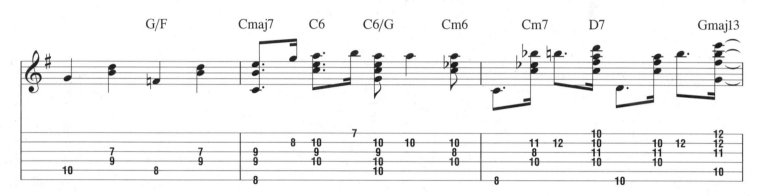

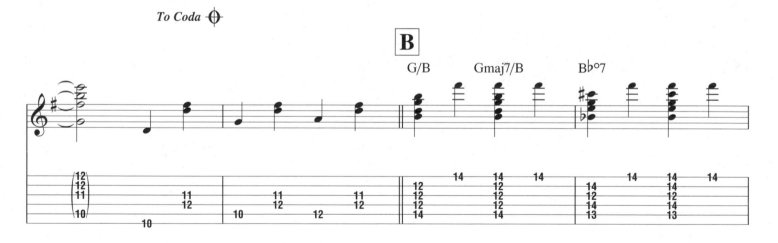

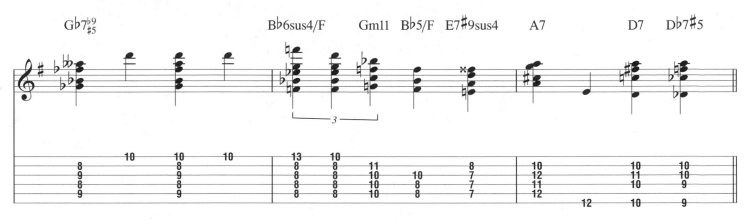

⊕ Coda

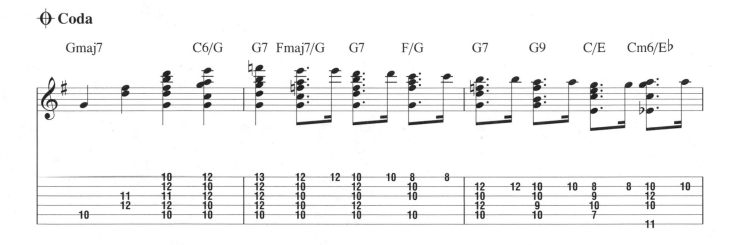

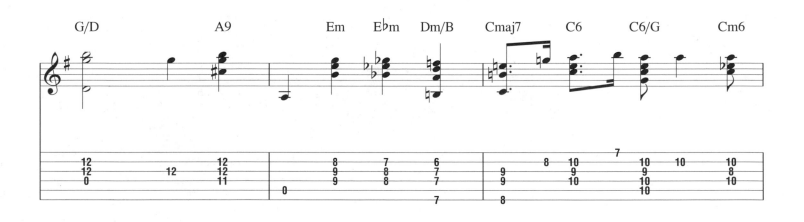

Let's Face the Music and Dance

from the Motion Picture FOLLOW THE FLEET
Words and Music by Irving Berlin

A

Moderately

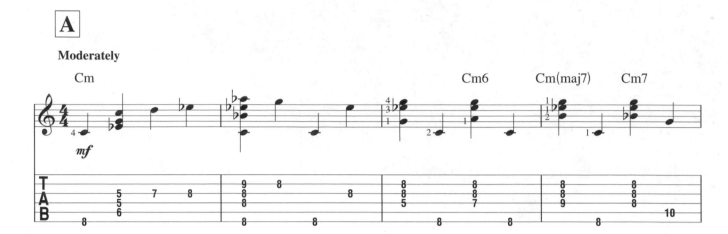

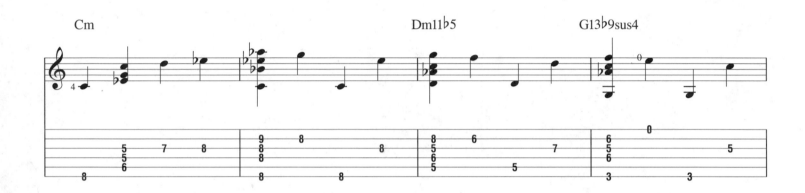

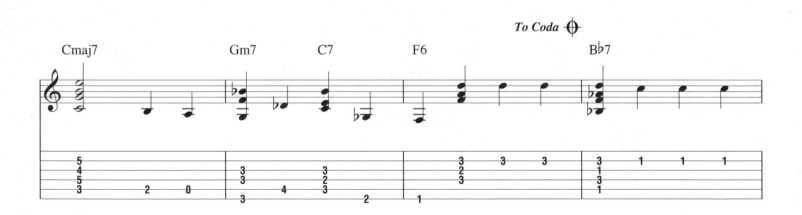

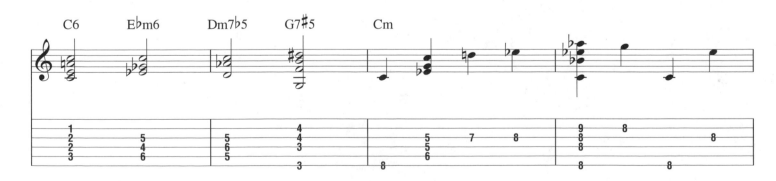

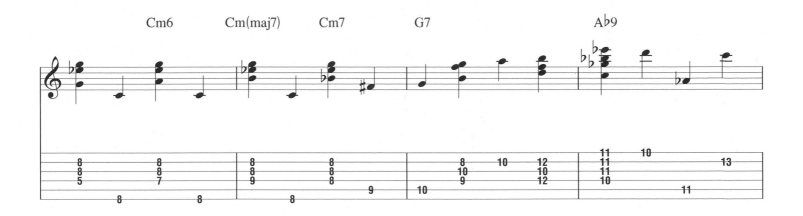

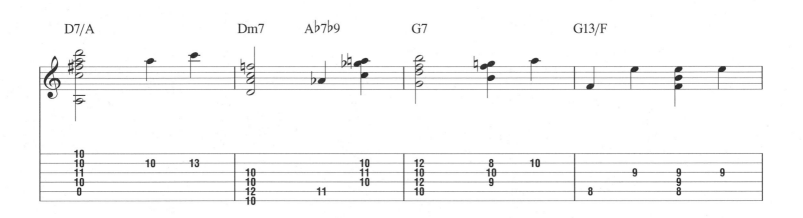

B

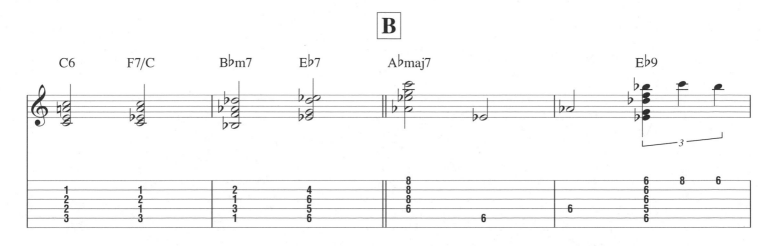

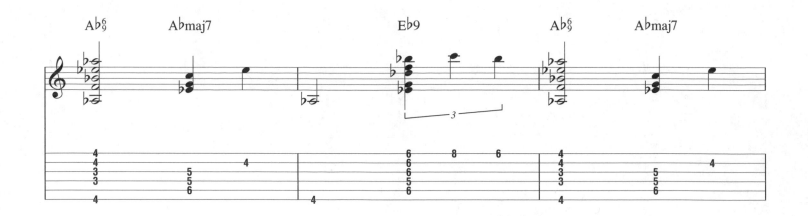

D.C. al Coda

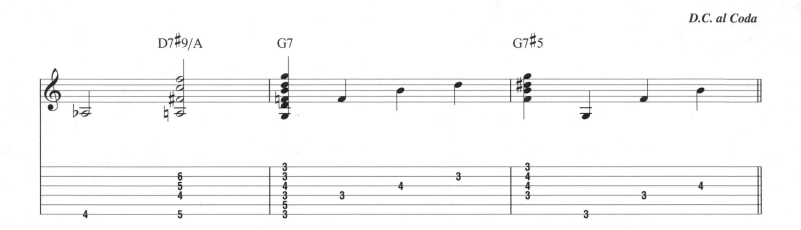

Coda

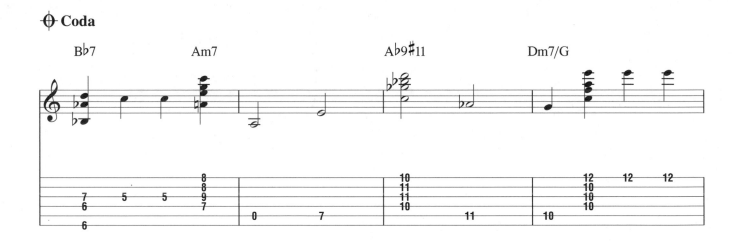

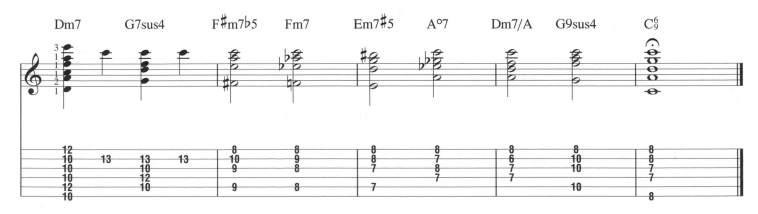

Puttin' on the Ritz

from the Motion Picture PUTTIN' ON THE RITZ

Words and Music by Irving Berlin

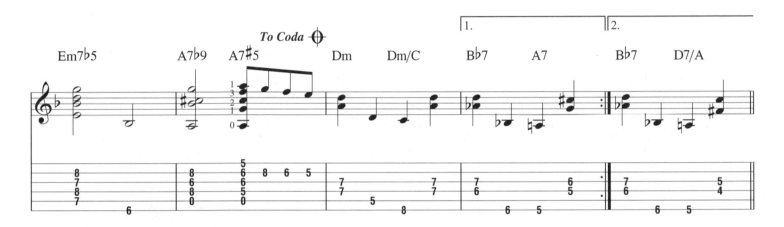

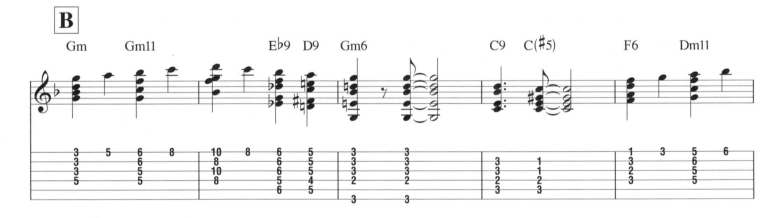

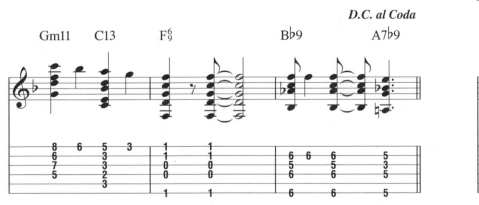

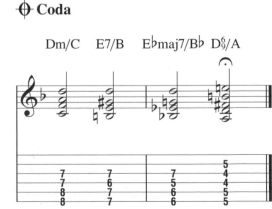

A Pretty Girl Is Like a Melody

from the 1919 Stage Production ZIEGFELD FOLLIES
from THE GREAT ZIEGFELD
Words and Music by Irving Berlin

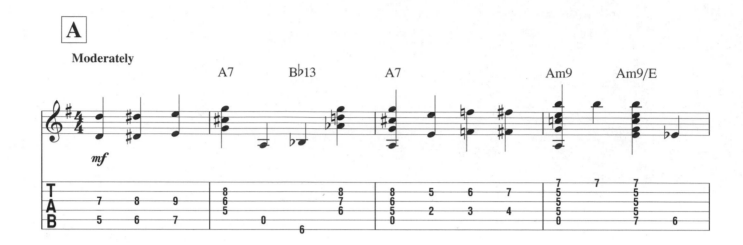

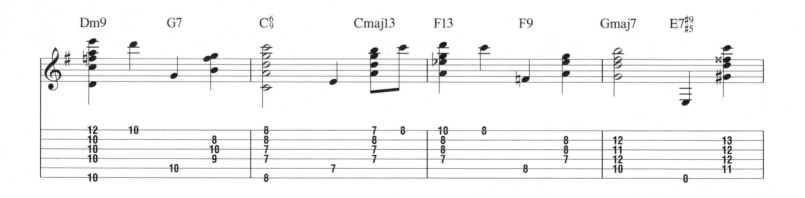

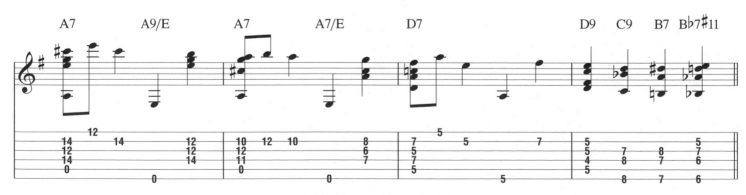

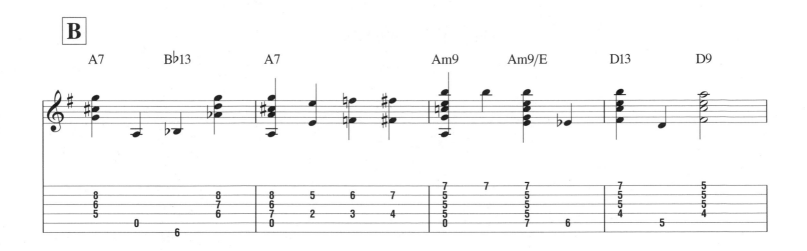

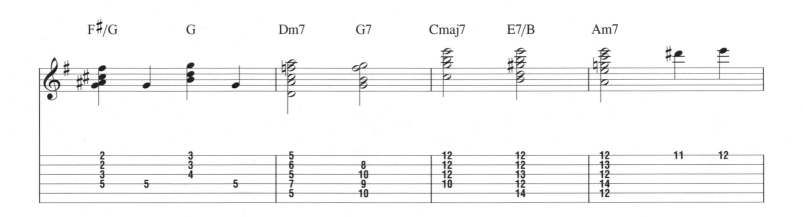

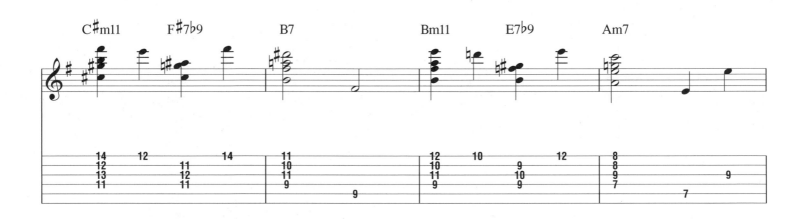

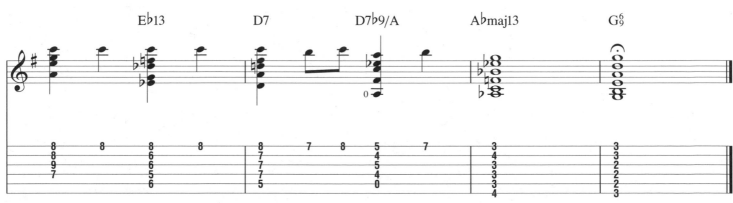

Remember

Words and Music by Irving Berlin

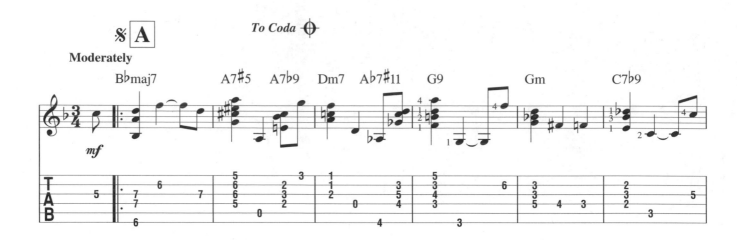

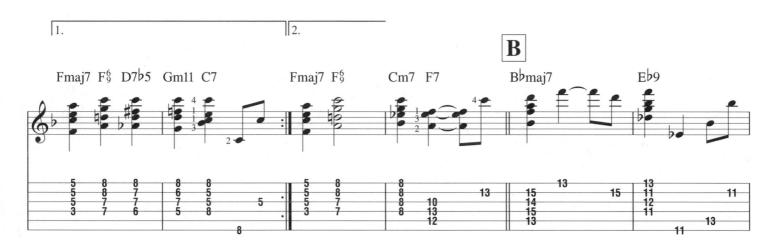

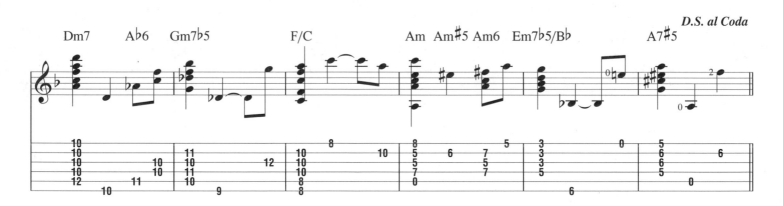

Say It with Music

from the 1921 Stage Production MUSIC BOX REVUE
from the 20th Century Fox Motion Picture
ALEXANDER'S RAGTIME BAND
Words and Music by Irving Berlin

Say It Isn't So

Words and Music by Irving Berlin

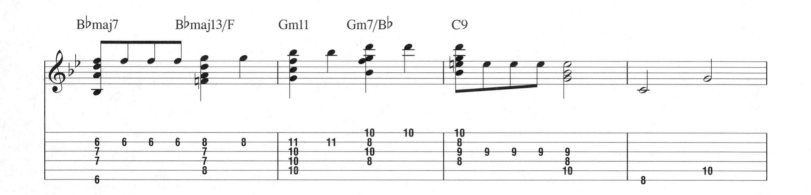

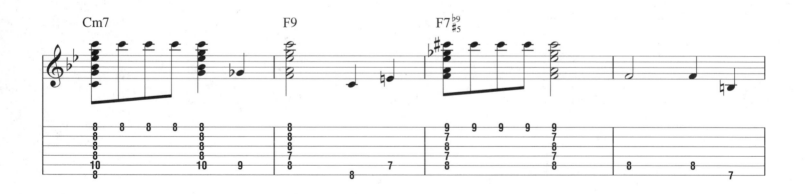

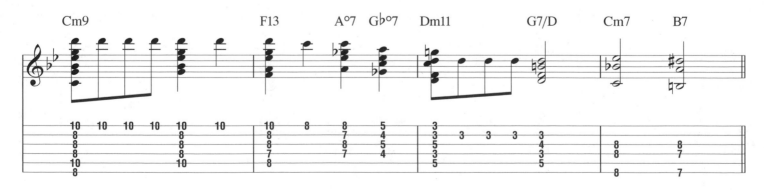

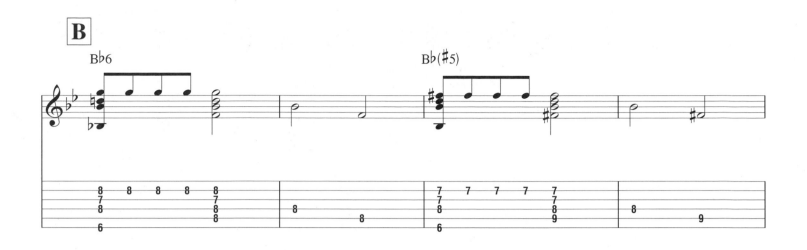

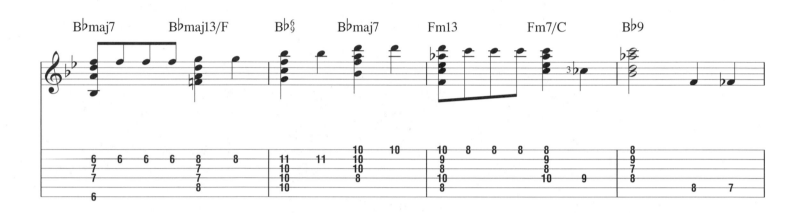

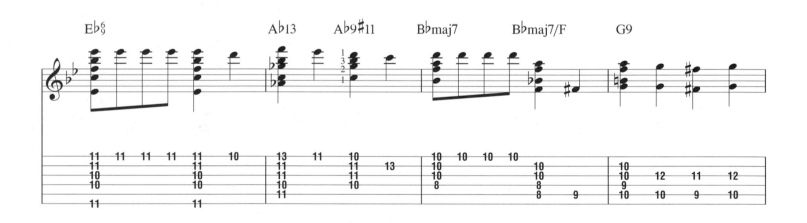

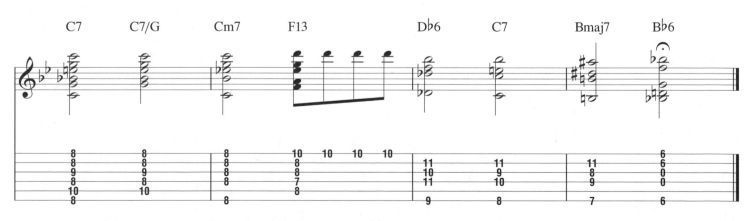

Soft Lights and Sweet Music

from the Stage Production FACE THE MUSIC
Words and Music by Irving Berlin

The Song Is Ended
(But the Melody Lingers On)

Words and Music by Irving Berlin

There's No Business Like
Show Business

from the Stage Production ANNIE GET YOUR GUN
Words and Music by Irving Berlin

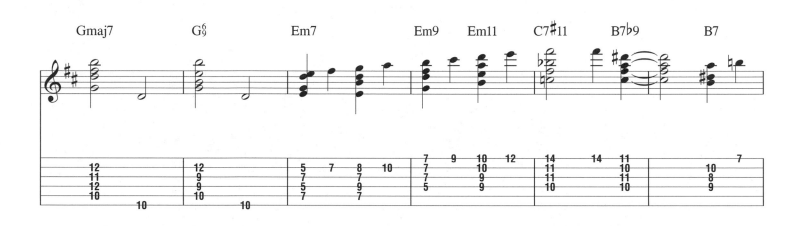

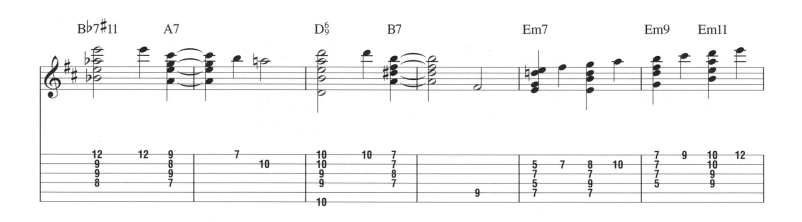

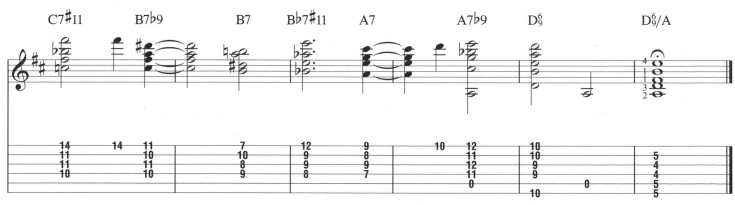

They Say It's Wonderful

from the Stage Production ANNIE GET YOUR GUN
Words and Music by Irving Berlin

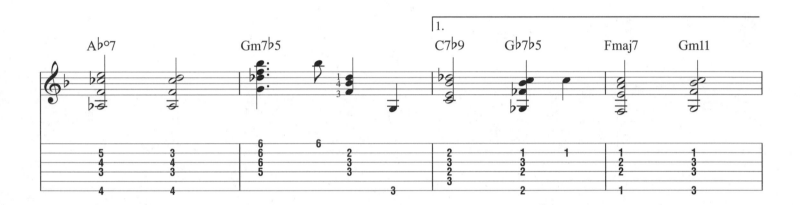

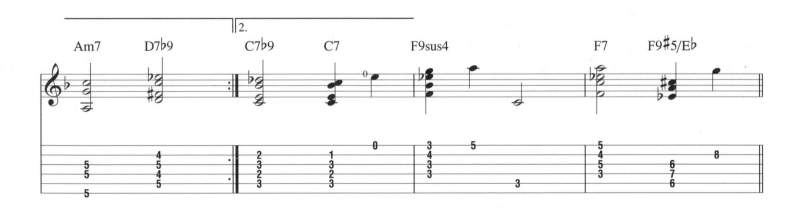

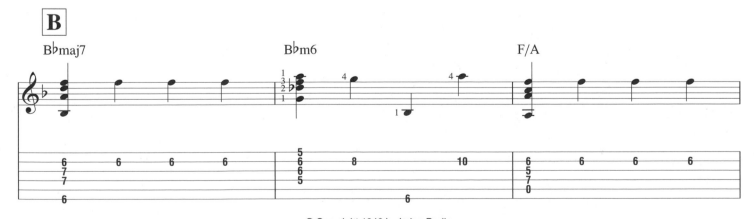

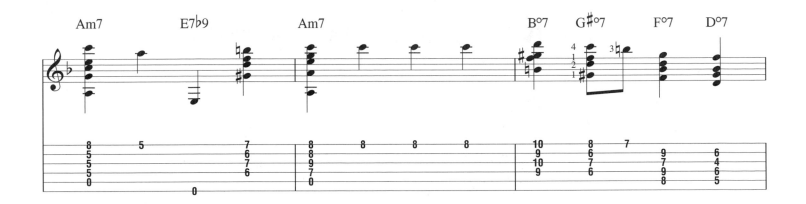

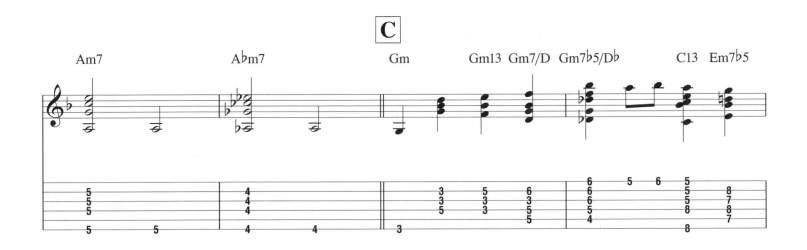

C

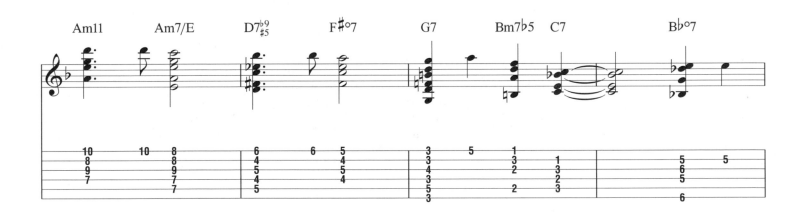

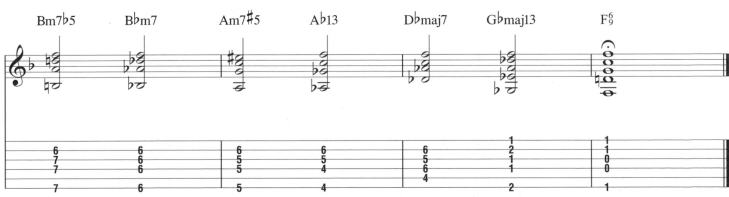

Steppin' Out with My Baby

from the Motion Picture Irving Berlin's EASTER PARADE
Words and Music by Irving Berlin

What'll I Do?

from MUSIC BOX REVUE OF 1924

Words and Music by Irving Berlin

White Christmas

from the Motion Picture Irving Berlin's HOLIDAY INN
Words and Music by Irving Berlin

A

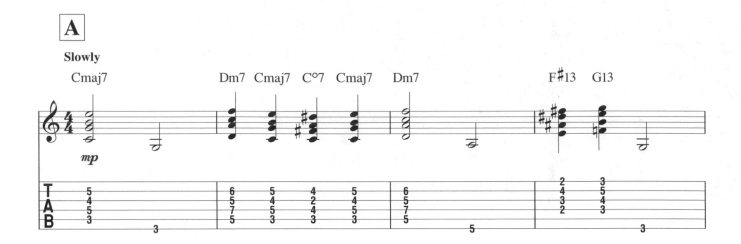

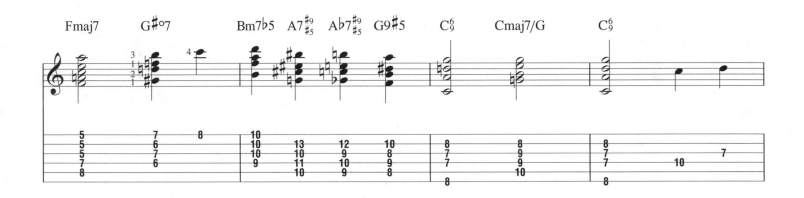

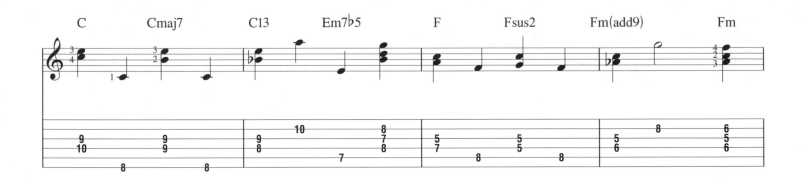

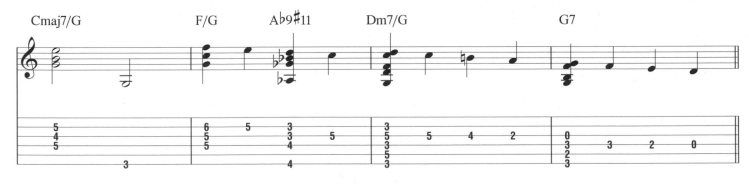

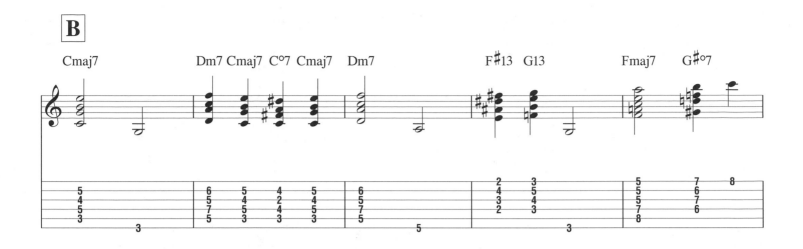

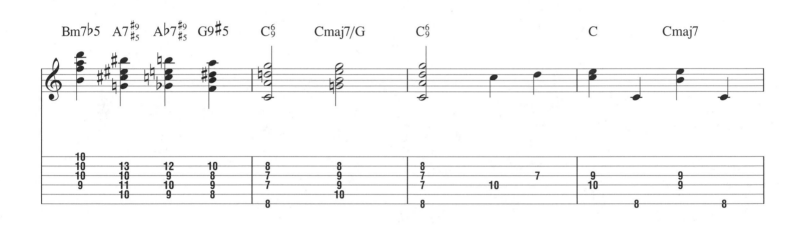

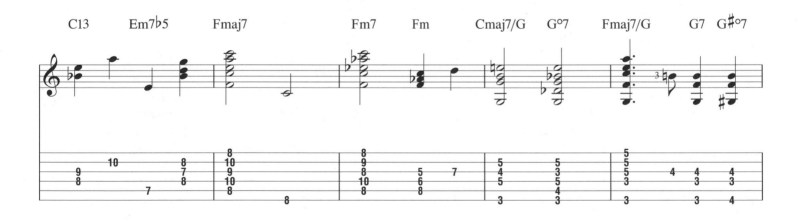

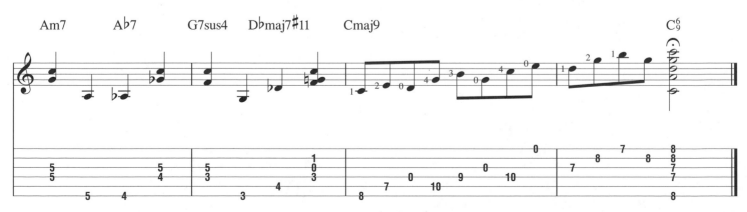

Guitar Notation Legend

THE MUSICAL STAFF shows pitches and rhythms and is divided by bar lines into measures. Pitches are named after the first seven letters of the alphabet.

TABLATURE graphically represents the guitar fingerboard. Each horizontal line represents a string, and each number represents a fret.

4th string, 2nd fret   1st & 2nd strings open, played together   open D chord

HALF-STEP BEND: Strike the note and bend up 1/2 step.

WHOLE-STEP BEND: Strike the note and bend up one step.

GRACE NOTE BEND: Strike the note and bend up as indicated. The first note does not take up any time.

SLIGHT (MICROTONE) BEND: Strike the note and bend up 1/4 step.

BEND AND RELEASE: Strike the note and bend up as indicated, then release back to the original note. Only the first note is struck.

PRE-BEND: Bend the note as indicated, then strike it.

VIBRATO: The string is vibrated by rapidly bending and releasing the note with the fretting hand.

PALM MUTING: The note is partially muted by the pick hand lightly touching the string(s) just before the bridge.

HAMMER-ON: Strike the first (lower) note with one finger, then sound the higher note (on the same string) with another finger by fretting it without picking.

PULL-OFF: Place both fingers on the notes to be sounded. Strike the first note and without picking, pull the finger off to sound the second (lower) note.

LEGATO SLIDE: Strike the first note and then slide the same fret-hand finger up or down to the second note. The second note is not struck.

SHIFT SLIDE: Same as legato slide, except the second note is struck.

PINCH HARMONIC: The note is fretted normally and a harmonic is produced by adding the edge of the thumb or the tip of the index finger of the pick hand to the normal pick attack.

TRILL: Very rapidly alternate between the notes indicated by continuously hammering on and pulling off.

TAPPING: Hammer ("tap") the fret indicated with the pick-hand index or middle finger and pull off to the note fretted by the fret hand.

NATURAL HARMONIC: Strike the note while the fret-hand lightly touches the string directly over the fret indicated.

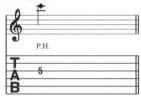

TREMOLO PICKING: The note is picked as rapidly and continuously as possible.

VIBRATO BAR DIVE AND RETURN: The pitch of the note or chord is dropped a specified number of steps (in rhythm) then returned to the original pitch.

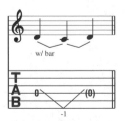

VIBRATO BAR SCOOP: Depress the bar just before striking the note, then quickly release the bar.

VIBRATO BAR DIP: Strike the note and then immediately drop a specified number of steps, then release back to the original pitch.

Additional Musical Definitions

(accent)   • Accentuate note (play it louder)

(staccato)   • Play the note short

D.S. al Coda   • Go back to the sign (𝄋), then play until the measure marked **"To Coda"**, then skip to the section labelled **"Coda."**

D.C. al Fine   • Go back to the beginning of the song and play until the measure marked **"Fine"** (end).

Fill   • Label used to identify a brief melodic figure which is to be inserted into the arrangement.

N.C.   • No Chord

• Repeat measures between signs.

• When a repeated section has different endings, play the first ending only the first time and the second ending only the second time.

52

FINGERPICKING
GUITAR BOOKS

Hone your fingerpicking skills with these great songbooks featuring solo guitar arrangements in standard notation and tablature. The arrangements in these books are carefully written for intermediate-level guitarists. Each song combines melody and harmony in one superb guitar fingerpicking arrangement. Each book also includes an introduction to basic fingerstyle guitar.

FINGERPICKING ACOUSTIC
15 songs: Behind Blue Eyes • Best of My Love • Blowin' in the Wind • The Boxer • Dust in the Wind • Helplessly Hoping • Hey Jude • In My Life • Learning to Fly • Leaving on a Jet Plane • Tears in Heaven • Time in a Bottle • You've Got a Friend • and more.
00699614..$9.99

FINGERPICKING ACOUSTIC ROCK
15 songs: American Pie • Bridge over Troubled Water • Every Rose Has Its Thorn • Knockin' on Heaven's Door • Landslide • More Than Words • Norwegian Wood (This Bird Has Flown) • Suite: Judy Blue Eyes • Wanted Dead or Alive • and more.
00699764..$9.99

FINGERPICKING BACH
12 masterpieces from J.S. Bach: Air on the G String • Bourrée in E Minor • Jesu, Joy of Man's Desiring • Little Prelude No. 2 in C Major • Minuet in G • Prelude in C Major • Quia Respexit • Sheep May Safely Graze • and more.
00699793..$8.95

FINGERPICKING BALLADS
15 songs: Against All Odds • (Everything I Do) I Do It for You • Fields of Gold • Have I Told You Lately • It's All Coming Back to Me Now • Looks Like We Made It • Rainy Days and Mondays • Say You, Say Me • She's Got a Way • Your Song • and more.
00699717..$9.99

FINGERPICKING BEATLES
30 songs including: All You Need Is Love • And I Love Her • Can't Buy Me Love • Hey Jude • In My Life • Lady Madonna • Let It Be • Love Me Do • Michelle • Nowhere Man • Please Please Me • Something • Ticket to Ride • Yellow Submarine • Yesterday • and more.
00699049..$19.95

FINGERPICKING CHILDREN'S SONGS
15 songs: Any Dream Will Do • Do-Re-Mi • It's a Small World • Linus and Lucy • The Muppet Show Theme • Puff the Magic Dragon • The Rainbow Connection • Sesame Street Theme • Winnie the Pooh • Zip-A-Dee-Doo-Dah • and more.
00699712..$9.99

FINGERPICKING CHRISTMAS
20 classic carols: Away in a Manger • Deck the Hall • The First Noel • God Rest Ye, Merry Gentlemen • Hark! The Herald Angels Sing • It Came Upon the Midnight Clear • Jingle Bells • O Little Town of Bethlehem • Silent Night • What Child Is This • and more.
00699599..$8.95

FINGERPICKING CLASSICAL
15 songs: Ave Maria • Bourée in E Minor • Canon in D • Eine Kleine Nachtmusik • Für Elise • Habanera • Minuet in G Major (Bach) • Minuet in G Major (Beethoven) • New World Symphony • Pomp and Circumstance • and more.
00699620..$8.95

FOR MORE INFORMATION, SEE YOUR LOCAL MUSIC DEALER,
OR WRITE TO:

HAL•LEONARD®
CORPORATION
7777 W. BLUEMOUND RD. P.O. BOX 13819 MILWAUKEE, WI 53213

Visit Hal Leonard online at **www.halleonard.com**

FINGERPICKING COUNTRY
17 classic favorites: Always on My Mind • By the Time I Get to Phoenix • Could I Have This Dance • Crazy • Green Green Grass of Home • He Stopped Loving Her Today • I Walk the Line • King of the Road • Tennessee Waltz • You Are My Sunshine • and more.
00699687..$9.99

FINGERPICKING DISNEY
15 songs: The Bare Necessities • Beauty and the Beast • Can You Feel the Love Tonight • Colors of the Wind • Go the Distance • If I Didn't Have You • Look Through My Eyes • Reflection • Under the Sea • A Whole New World • You'll Be in My Heart • and more.
00699711..$9.95

FINGERPICKING HYMNS
15 songs: Amazing Grace • Beneath the Cross of Jesus • Come, Thou Fount of Every Blessing • For the Beauty of the Earth • I've Got Peace like a River • Jacob's Ladder • A Mighty Fortress Is Our God • Rock of Ages • and more.
00699688..$8.95

FINGERPICKING ANDREW LLOYD WEBBER
14 songs: All I Ask of You • Don't Cry for Me Argentina • Memory • The Music of the Night • With One Look • more.
00699839..$9.99

FINGERPICKING MOZART
15 of Mozart's timeless compositions: Ave Verum • Eine Kleine Nachtmusik • Laudate Dominum • Minuet in G Major, K. 1 • Piano Concerto No. 21 in C Major • Piano Sonata in A • Piano Sonata in C • Rondo in C Major • and more.
00699794..$8.95

FINGERPICKING POP
Includes 15 songs: Can You Feel the Love Tonight • Don't Know Why • Endless Love • Imagine • Let It Be • My Cherie Amour • My Heart Will Go On • Piano Man • Stand by Me • We've Only Just Begun • Wonderful Tonight • and more.
00699615..$9.99

FINGERPICKING PRAISE
15 songs: Above All • Breathe • Draw Me Close • Great Is the Lord • He Is Exalted • Jesus, Name Above All Names • Oh Lord, You're Beautiful • Open the Eyes of My Heart • Shine, Jesus, Shine • Shout to the Lord • You Are My King • and more.
00699714..$8.95

FINGERPICKING ROCK
15 songs: Abracadabra • Brown Eyed Girl • Crocodile Rock • Free Bird • The House of the Rising Sun • I Want You to Want Me • Livin' on a Prayer • Maggie May • Rhiannon • Still the Same • When the Children Cry • and more.
00699716..$9.99

FINGERPICKING STANDARDS
17 fantastic songs: Can't Help Falling in Love • Fly Me to the Moon • Georgia on My Mind • I Just Called to Say I Love You • Just the Way You Are • Misty • Moon River • Unchained Melody • What a Wonderful World • When I Fall in Love • Yesterday • and more.
00699613..$9.99

FINGERPICKING WEDDING
15 tunes for the big day: Beautiful in My Eyes • Don't Know Much • Endless Love • Grow Old with Me • In My Life • The Lord's Prayer • This Is the Day (A Wedding Song) • We've Only Just Begun • Wedding Processional • You and I • and more.
00699637..$9.99

FINGERPICKING YULETIDE
16 holiday favorites: Blue Christmas • The Christmas Song • Frosty the Snow Man • A Holly Jolly Christmas • I'll Be Home for Christmas • Jingle-Bell Rock • Let It Snow! Let It Snow! Let It Snow! • Merry Christmas, Darling • Rudolph the Red-Nosed Reindeer • and more.
00699654..$9.99

Prices, contents and availability subject to change without notice.

GUITAR RECORDED VERSIONS®

AUTHENTIC TRANSCRIPTIONS WITH NOTES AND TABLATURE

Guitar Recorded Versions® are note-for-note transcriptions of guitar music taken directly off recordings. This series, one of the most popular in print today, features some of the greatest guitar players and groups from blues and rock to country and jazz.

Guitar Recorded Versions are transcribed by the best transcribers in the business. Every book contains notes and tablature. Visit www.halleonard.com for our complete selection.

00690501	Bryan Adams – Greatest Hits	$19.95
00690002	Aerosmith – Big Ones	$24.95
00692015	Aerosmith – Greatest Hits	$22.95
00690603	Aerosmith – O Yeah! (Ultimate Hits)	$24.95
00690147	Aerosmith – Rocks	$19.95
00690139	Alice in Chains	$19.95
00690178	Alice in Chains – Acoustic	$19.95
00694865	Alice in Chains – Dirt	$19.95
00660225	Alice in Chains – Facelift	$19.95
00694925	Alice in Chains – Jar of Flies/Sap	$19.95
00690387	Alice in Chains – Nothing Safe: Best of the Box	$19.95
00690899	All That Remains – The Fall of Ideals	$19.95
00690812	All-American Rejects – Move Along	$19.95
00694932	Allman Brothers Band – Definitive Collection for Guitar Volume 1	$24.95
00694933	Allman Brothers Band – Definitive Collection for Guitar Volume 2	$24.95
00694934	Allman Brothers Band – Definitive Collection for Guitar Volume 3	$24.95
00690755	Alter Bridge – One Day Remains	$19.95
00690571	Trey Anastasio	$19.95
00690158	Chet Atkins – Almost Alone	$19.95
00694876	Chet Atkins – Contemporary Styles	$19.95
00694878	Chet Atkins – Vintage Fingerstyle	$19.95
00690865	Atreyu – A Deathgrip on Yesterday	$19.95
00690609	Audioslave	$19.95
00690804	Audioslave – Out of Exile	$19.95
00690926	Avenged Sevenfold	$22.95
00690884	Audioslave – Revelations	$19.95
00690820	Avenged Sevenfold – City of Evil	$24.95
00694918	Randy Bachman Collection	$22.95
00690366	Bad Company – Original Anthology – Book 1	$19.95
00690367	Bad Company – Original Anthology – Book 2	$19.95
00690503	Beach Boys – Very Best of	$19.95
00694929	Beatles: 1962-1966	$24.95
00694930	Beatles: 1967-1970	$24.95
00690489	Beatles – 1	$24.95
00694880	Beatles – Abbey Road	$19.95
00690110	Beatles – Book 1 (White Album)	$19.95
00690111	Beatles – Book 2 (White Album)	$19.95
00694832	Beatles – For Acoustic Guitar	$22.95
00690137	Beatles – A Hard Day's Night	$16.95
00690482	Beatles – Let It Be	$17.95
00694891	Beatles – Revolver	$19.95
00694914	Beatles – Rubber Soul	$19.95
00694863	Beatles – Sgt. Pepper's Lonely Hearts Club Band	$19.95
00690383	Beatles – Yellow Submarine	$19.95
00690175	Beck – Odelay	$17.95
00690632	Beck – Sea Change	$19.95
00694884	Best of George Benson	$19.95
00692385	Chuck Berry	$19.95
00690835	Billy Talent	$19.95
00690879	Billy Talent II	$19.95
00690149	Black Sabbath	$14.95
00690901	Best of Black Sabbath	$19.95
00690148	Black Sabbath – Master of Reality	$14.95
00690142	Black Sabbath – Paranoid	$14.95
00692200	Black Sabbath – We Sold Our Soul for Rock 'N' Roll	$19.95
00690674	blink-182	$19.95
00690389	blink-182 – Enema of the State	$19.95
00690831	blink-182 – Greatest Hits	$19.95
00690523	blink-182 – Take Off Your Pants and Jacket	$19.95
00690028	Blue Oyster Cult – Cult Classics	$19.95
00690851	James Blunt – Back to Bedlam	$22.95
00690008	Bon Jovi – Cross Road	$19.95
00690913	Boston	$19.95
00690932	Boston – Don't Look Back	$19.99
00690491	Best of David Bowie	$19.95
00690583	Box Car Racer	$19.95
00690873	Breaking Benjamin – Phobia	$19.95
00690764	Breaking Benjamin – We Are Not Alone	$19.95
00690451	Jeff Buckley Collection	$24.95
00690678	Best of Kenny Burrell	$19.95
00690564	The Calling – Camino Palmero	$19.95
00690261	Carter Family Collection	$19.95
00690293	Best of Steven Curtis Chapman	$19.95
00690043	Best of Cheap Trick	$19.95
00690171	Chicago – The Definitive Guitar Collection	$22.95
00690567	Charlie Christian – The Definitive Collection	$19.95
00690590	Eric Clapton – Anthology	$29.95
00692391	Best of Eric Clapton – 2nd Edition	$22.95
00690393	Eric Clapton – Selections from Blues	$19.95
00690936	Eric Clapton – Complete Clapton	$29.95
00690074	Eric Clapton – Cream of Clapton	$24.95
00690010	Eric Clapton – From the Cradle	$19.95
00690716	Eric Clapton – Me and Mr. Johnson	$19.95
00690263	Eric Clapton – Slowhand	$19.95
00694873	Eric Clapton – Timepieces	$19.95
00694869	Eric Clapton – Unplugged	$22.95
00690415	Clapton Chronicles – Best of Eric Clapton	$18.95
00694896	John Mayall/Eric Clapton – Bluesbreakers	$19.95
00690162	Best of the Clash	$19.95
00690828	Coheed & Cambria – Good Apollo I'm Burning Star, IV, Vol. 1: From Fear Through the Eyes of Madness	$19.95
00690940	Coheed and Cambria – No World for Tomorrow	$19.95
00690494	Coldplay – Parachutes	$19.95
00690593	Coldplay – A Rush of Blood to the Head	$19.95
00690906	Coldplay – The Singles & B-Sides	$24.95
00690962	Coldplay – Viva La Vida	$19.95
00690806	Coldplay – X & Y	$19.95
00690855	Best of Collective Soul	$19.95
00690928	Chris Cornell – Carry On	$19.95
00694940	Counting Crows – August & Everything After	$19.95
00690405	Counting Crows – This Desert Life	$19.95
00694840	Cream – Disraeli Gears	$19.95
00690285	Cream – Those Were the Days	$17.95
00690352	Creed – My Own Prison	$19.95
00690551	Creed – Weathered	$19.95
00690819	Best of Creedence Clearwater Revival	$22.95
00690648	The Very Best of Jim Croce	$19.95
00690572	Steve Cropper – Soul Man	$19.95
00690613	Best of Crosby, Stills & Nash	$22.95
00690777	Crossfade	$19.95
00699521	The Cure – Greatest Hits	$24.95
00690637	Best of Dick Dale	$19.95
00690882	Dashboard Confessional – Dusk and Summer	$19.95
00690892	Daughtry	$19.95
00690967	Death Cab for Cutie – Narrow Stairs	$22.99
00690822	Best of Alex De Grassi	$19.95
00690289	Best of Deep Purple	$17.95
00690784	Best of Def Leppard	$19.95
00694831	Derek and the Dominos – Layla & Other Assorted Love Songs	$22.95
00690384	Best of Ani DiFranco	$19.95
00690322	Ani DiFranco – Little Plastic Castle	$19.95
00695382	Very Best of Dire Straits – Sultans of Swing	$19.95
00690347	The Doors – Anthology	$22.95
00690348	The Doors – Essential Guitar Collection	$16.95
00690915	Dragonforce – Inhuman Rampage	$29.95
00690250	Best of Duane Eddy	$16.95
00690533	Electric Light Orchestra Guitar Collection	$19.95
00690909	Best of Tommy Emmanuel	$19.95
00690555	Best of Melissa Etheridge	$19.95
00690524	Melissa Etheridge – Skin	$19.95
00690496	Best of Everclear	$19.95
00690515	Extreme II – Pornograffitti	$19.95
00690810	Fall Out Boy – From Under the Cork Tree	$19.95
00690897	Fall Out Boy – Infinity on High	$22.95
00690664	Best of Fleetwood Mac	$19.95
00690870	Flyleaf	$19.95
00690257	John Fogerty – Blue Moon Swamp	$19.95
00690235	Foo Fighters – The Colour and the Shape	$19.95
00690808	Foo Fighters – In Your Honor	$19.95
00690595	Foo Fighters – One by One	$19.95
00690394	Foo Fighters – There Is Nothing Left to Lose	$19.95
00690805	Best of Robben Ford	$19.95
00690842	Best of Peter Frampton	$19.95
00690734	Franz Ferdinand	$19.95
00694920	Best of Free	$19.95
00690222	G3 Live – Joe Satriani, Steve Vai, and Eric Johnson	$22.95
00694807	Danny Gatton – 88 Elmira St	$19.95
00690438	Genesis Guitar Anthology	$19.95
00690753	Best of Godsmack	$19.95
00120167	Godsmack	$19.95
00690848	Godsmack – IV	$19.95
00690338	Goo Goo Dolls – Dizzy Up the Girl	$19.95
00690576	Goo Goo Dolls – Gutterflower	$19.95
00690773	Good Charlotte – Chronicles of Life and Death	$19.95
00690601	Good Charlotte – The Young and the Hopeless	$19.95
00690117	John Gorka Collection	$19.95
00690591	Patty Griffin – Guitar Collection	$19.95
00690114	Buddy Guy Collection Vol. A-J	$22.95
00694854	Buddy Guy – Damn Right, I've Got the Blues	$19.95
00690697	Best of Jim Hall	$19.95
00690840	Ben Harper – Both Sides of the Gun	$19.95
00694798	George Harrison Anthology	$19.95
00690778	Hawk Nelson – Letters to the President	$19.95
00692930	Jimi Hendrix – Are You Experienced?	$24.95
00692931	Jimi Hendrix – Axis: Bold As Love	$22.95
00690304	Jimi Hendrix – Band of Gypsys	$22.95
00690321	Jimi Hendrix – BBC Sessions	$22.95
00690608	Jimi Hendrix – Blue Wild Angel	$24.95
00694944	Jimi Hendrix – Blues	$24.95
00692932	Jimi Hendrix – Electric Ladyland	$24.95
00690602	Jimi Hendrix – Smash Hits	$19.95
00690017	Jimi Hendrix – Woodstock	$24.95
00690843	H.I.M. – Dark Light	$19.95
00690869	Hinder – Extreme Behavior	$19.95
00660029	Buddy Holly	$19.95
00660169	John Lee Hooker – A Blues Legend	$19.95
00694905	Howlin' Wolf	$19.95
00690692	Very Best of Billy Idol	$19.95
00690688	Incubus – A Crow Left of the Murder	$19.95
00690457	Incubus – Make Yourself	$19.95
00690544	Incubus – Morningview	$19.95
00690136	Indigo Girls – 1200 Curfews	$22.95
00690790	Iron Maiden Anthology	$24.95
00690887	Iron Maiden – A Matter of Life and Death	$24.95
00690730	Alan Jackson – Guitar Collection	$19.95
00694938	Elmore James – Master Electric Slide Guitar	$19.95
00690652	Best of Jane's Addiction	$19.95
00690721	Jet – Get Born	$19.95
00690684	Jethro Tull – Aqualung	$19.95
00690647	Best of Jewel	$19.95
00690898	John 5 – The Devil Knows My Name	$22.95
00690959	John 5 – Requiem	$22.95
00690814	John 5 – Songs for Sanity	$19.95
00690751	John 5 – Vertigo	$19.95
00694912	Eric Johnson – Ah Via Musicom	$19.95
00690660	Best of Eric Johnson	$19.95
00690845	Eric Johnson – Bloom	$19.95
00690169	Eric Johnson – Venus Isle	$22.95
00690846	Jack Johnson and Friends – Sing-A-Longs and Lullabies for the Film Curious George	$19.95
00690271	Robert Johnson – The New Transcriptions	$24.95
00699131	Best of Janis Joplin	$19.95
00690427	Best of Judas Priest	$19.95
00690651	Juanes – Exitos de Juanes	$19.95
00690277	Best of Kansas	$19.95
00690742	The Killers – Hot Fuss	$19.95
00690888	The Killers – Sam's Town	$19.95
00690504	Very Best of Albert King	$19.95
00690444	B.B. King & Eric Clapton – Riding with the King	$19.95
00690134	Freddie King Collection	$19.95
00690339	Best of the Kinks	$19.95
00690157	Kiss – Alive!	$19.95

00694903	Best of Kiss for Guitar	$24.95
00690355	Kiss – Destroyer	$16.95
00690164	Mark Knopfler Guitar – Vol. 1	$19.95
00690163	Mark Knopfler/Chet Atkins – Neck and Neck	$19.95
00690780	Korn – Greatest Hits, Volume 1	$22.95
00690836	Korn – See You on the Other Side	$19.95
00690377	Kris Kristofferson Collection	$19.95
00690861	Kutless – Hearts of the Innocent	$19.95
00690834	Lamb of God – Ashes of the Wake	$19.95
00690875	Lamb of God – Sacrament	$19.95
00690890	Ray LaMontagne – Till the Sun Turns Black	$19.95
00690823	Ray LaMontagne – Trouble	$19.95
00690658	Johnny Lang – Long Time Coming	$19.95
00690726	Avril Lavigne – Under My Skin	$19.95
00690679	John Lennon – Guitar Collection	$19.95
00690279	Ottmar Liebert + Luna Negra – Opium Highlights	$19.95
00690782	Linkin Park – Meteora	$22.95
00690922	Linkin Park – Minutes to Midnight	$19.95
00690743	Los Lonely Boys	$19.95
00690720	Lostprophets – Start Something	$19.95
00690525	Best of George Lynch	$22.95
00694954	New Best of Lynyrd Skynyrd	$19.95
00690577	Yngwie Malmsteen – Anthology	$24.95
00694845	Yngwie Malmsteen – Fire and Ice	$19.95
00694755	Yngwie Malmsteen's Rising Force	$19.95
00694757	Yngwie Malmsteen – Trilogy	$19.95
00690754	Marilyn Manson – Lest We Forget	$19.95
00694956	Bob Marley – Legend	$19.95
00690548	Very Best of Bob Marley & The Wailers – One Love	$19.95
00694945	Bob Marley – Songs of Freedom	$24.95
00690914	Maroon 5 – It Won't Be Soon Before Long	$19.95
00690657	Maroon 5 – Songs About Jane	$19.95
00690442	Matchbox 20 – Mad Season	$19.95
00690239	Matchbox 20 – Yourself or Someone like You	$19.95
00690382	Sarah McLachlan – Mirrorball	$19.95
00694952	Megadeth – Countdown to Extinction	$22.95
00690244	Megadeth – Cryptic Writings	$19.95
00694951	Megadeth – Rust in Peace	$22.95
00690011	Megadeth – Youthanasia	$19.95
00690505	John Mellencamp Guitar Collection	$19.95
00690562	Pat Metheny – Bright Size Life	$19.95
00690646	Pat Metheny – One Quiet Night	$19.95
00690559	Pat Metheny – Question & Answer	$19.95
00690040	Steve Miller Band Greatest Hits	$19.95
00690769	Modest Mouse – Good News for People Who Love Bad News	$19.95
00694802	Gary Moore – Still Got the Blues	$19.95
00690103	Alanis Morissette – Jagged Little Pill	$19.95
00690787	Mudvayne – L.D. 50	$22.95
00690500	Ricky Nelson Guitar Collection	$17.95
00690722	New Found Glory – Catalyst	$19.95
00690880	New Found Glory – Coming Home	$19.95
00690924	The Nightwatchman – One Man Revolution	$19.95
00690611	Nirvana	$22.95
00694895	Nirvana – Bleach	$19.95
00690189	Nirvana – From the Muddy Banks of the Wishkah	$19.95
00694913	Nirvana – In Utero	$19.95
00694901	Nirvana – Incesticide	$19.95
00694883	Nirvana – Nevermind	$19.95
00690026	Nirvana – Unplugged in New York	$19.95
00120112	No Doubt – Tragic Kingdom	$22.95
00690121	Oasis – (What's the Story) Morning Glory	$19.95
00690226	Oasis – The Other Side of Oasis	$19.95
00690358	The Offspring – Americana	$19.95
00690485	The Offspring – Conspiracy of One	$19.95
00690204	The Offspring – Ixnay on the Hombre	$17.95
00690203	The Offspring – Smash	$18.95
00690818	The Best of Opeth	$22.95
00694847	Best of Ozzy Osbourne	$22.95
00690921	Ozzy Osbourne – Black Rain	$19.95

00694830	Ozzy Osbourne – No More Tears	$19.95
00690399	Ozzy Osbourne – The Ozzman Cometh	$19.95
00690129	Ozzy Osbourne – Ozzmosis	$22.95
00690933	Best of Brad Paisley	$22.95
00690866	Panic! At the Disco – A Fever You Can't Sweat Out	$19.95
00690885	Papa Roach – The Paramour Sessions	$19.95
00690594	Best of Les Paul	$19.95
00690546	P.O.D. – Satellite	$19.95
00694855	Pearl Jam – Ten	$19.95
00690439	A Perfect Circle – Mer De Noms	$19.95
00690661	A Perfect Circle – Thirteenth Step	$19.95
00690499	Tom Petty – Definitive Guitar Collection	$19.95
00690868	Tom Petty – Highway Companion	$19.95
00690176	Phish – Billy Breathes	$22.95
00690331	Phish – Story of the Ghost	$19.95
00690428	Pink Floyd – Dark Side of the Moon	$19.95
00690789	Best of Poison	$19.95
00693864	Best of The Police	$19.95
00690299	Best of Elvis: The King of Rock 'n' Roll	$19.95
00692535	Elvis Presley	$19.95
00690003	Classic Queen	$24.95
00694975	Queen – Greatest Hits	$24.95
00690670	Very Best of Queensryche	$19.95
00690878	The Raconteurs – Broken Boy Soldiers	$19.95
00694910	Rage Against the Machine	$19.95
00690179	Rancid – And Out Come the Wolves	$22.95
00690426	Best of Ratt	$19.95
00690055	Red Hot Chili Peppers – Blood Sugar Sex Magik	$19.95
00690584	Red Hot Chili Peppers – By the Way	$19.95
00690379	Red Hot Chili Peppers – Californication	$19.95
00690673	Red Hot Chili Peppers – Greatest Hits	$19.95
00690090	Red Hot Chili Peppers – One Hot Minute	$22.95
00690852	Red Hot Chili Peppers – Stadium Arcadium	$24.95
00690893	The Red Jumpsuit Apparatus – Don't You Fake It	$19.95
00690511	Django Reinhardt – The Definitive Collection	$19.95
00690779	Relient K – MMHMM	$19.95
00690643	Relient K – Two Lefts Don't Make a Right ... But Three Do	$19.95
00694899	R.E.M. – Automatic for the People	$19.95
00690260	Jimmie Rodgers Guitar Collection	$19.95
00690014	Rolling Stones – Exile on Main Street	$24.95
00690631	Rolling Stones – Guitar Anthology	$27.95
00690685	David Lee Roth – Eat 'Em and Smile	$19.95
00690031	Santana's Greatest Hits	$19.95
00690796	Very Best of Michael Schenker	$19.95
00690566	Best of Scorpions	$19.95
00690604	Bob Seger – Guitar Anthology	$19.95
00690659	Bob Seger and the Silver Bullet Band – Greatest Hits, Volume 2	$17.95
00690896	Shadows Fall – Threads of Life	$19.95
00690803	Best of Kenny Wayne Shepherd Band	$19.95
00690750	Kenny Wayne Shepherd – The Place You're In	$19.95
00690857	Shinedown – Us and Them	$19.95
00690196	Silverchair – Freak Show	$19.95
00690130	Silverchair – Frogstomp	$19.95
00690872	Slayer – Christ Illusion	$19.95
00690813	Slayer – Guitar Collection	$19.95
00690419	Slipknot	$19.95
00690973	Slipknot – All Hope Is Gone	$22.99
00690530	Slipknot – Iowa	$19.95
00690733	Slipknot – Volume 3 (The Subliminal Verses)	$22.99
00690330	Social Distortion – Live at the Roxy	$19.95
00120004	Best of Steely Dan	$24.95
00694921	Best of Steppenwolf	$22.95
00690655	Best of Mike Stern	$19.95
00690021	Sting – Fields of Gold	$19.95
00690597	Stone Sour	$19.95
00690689	Story of the Year – Page Avenue	$19.95
00690520	Styx Guitar Collection	$19.95
00120081	Sublime	$19.95
00690519	SUM 41 – All Killer No Filler	$19.95
00690767	Switchfoot – The Beautiful Letdown	$19.95

00690425	System of a Down	$19.95
00690830	System of a Down – Hypnotize	$19.95
00690799	System of a Down – Mezmerize	$19.95
00690531	System of a Down – Toxicity	$19.95
00694824	Best of James Taylor	$16.95
00694887	Best of Thin Lizzy	$19.95
00690825	Third Day – Wherever You Are	$19.95
00690671	Three Days Grace	$19.95
00690871	Three Days Grace – One-X	$19.95
00690737	3 Doors Down – The Better Life	$22.95
00690891	30 Seconds to Mars – A Beautiful Lie	$19.95
00690269	311 – Grass Roots	$19.95
00690665	Thursday – War All the Time	$19.95
00690030	Toad the Wet Sprocket	$19.95
00690654	Best of Train	$19.95
00690683	Robin Trower – Bridge of Sighs	$19.95
00699191	U2 – Best of: 1980-1990	$19.95
00690732	U2 – Best of: 1990-2000	$19.95
00690894	U2 – 18 Singles	$19.95
00690775	U2 – How to Dismantle an Atomic Bomb	$22.95
00690039	Steve Vai – Alien Love Secrets	$24.95
00690172	Steve Vai – Fire Garden	$24.95
00660137	Steve Vai – Passion & Warfare	$24.95
00690881	Steve Vai – Real Illusions: Reflections	$24.95
00694904	Steve Vai – Sex and Religion	$24.95
00690392	Steve Vai – The Ultra Zone	$19.95
00690024	Stevie Ray Vaughan – Couldn't Stand the Weather	$19.95
00690370	Stevie Ray Vaughan and Double Trouble – The Real Deal: Greatest Hits Volume 2	$22.95
00690116	Stevie Ray Vaughan – Guitar Collection	$24.95
00660136	Stevie Ray Vaughan – In Step	$19.95
00694879	Stevie Ray Vaughan – In the Beginning	$19.95
00660058	Stevie Ray Vaughan – Lightnin' Blues '83-'87	$24.95
00690036	Stevie Ray Vaughan – Live Alive	$24.95
00694835	Stevie Ray Vaughan – The Sky Is Crying	$22.95
00690025	Stevie Ray Vaughan – Soul to Soul	$19.95
00690015	Stevie Ray Vaughan – Texas Flood	$19.95
00694776	Vaughan Brothers – Family Style	$19.95
00690772	Velvet Revolver – Contraband	$22.95
00690920	Velvet Revolver – Libertad	$19.95
00690132	The T-Bone Walker Collection	$19.95
00694789	Muddy Waters – Deep Blues	$24.95
00690071	Weezer (The Blue Album)	$19.95
00690516	Weezer (The Green Album)	$19.95
00690286	Weezer – Pinkerton	$19.95
00690447	Best of the Who	$24.95
00694970	The Who – Definitive Guitar Collection: A-E	$24.95
00694971	The Who – Definitive Guitar Collection F-Li	$24.95
00694972	The Who – Definitive Guitar Collection: Lo-R	$24.95
00694973	The Who – Definitive Guitar Collection: S-Y	$24.95
00690672	Best of Dar Williams	$19.95
00690320	Dar Williams Songbook	$19.95
00690319	Stevie Wonder – Some of the Best	$17.95
00690596	Best of the Yardbirds	$19.95
00690696	Yeah Yeah Yeahs – Fever to Tell	$19.95
00690844	Yellowcard – Lights and Sounds	$19.95
00690916	The Best of Dwight Yoakam	$19.95
00690904	Neil Young – Harvest	$19.95
00690443	Frank Zappa – Hot Rats	$19.95
00690623	Frank Zappa – Over-Nite Sensation	$19.95
00690589	ZZ Top – Guitar Anthology	$24.95

FOR MORE INFORMATION, SEE YOUR LOCAL MUSIC DEALER, OR WRITE TO:

HAL•LEONARD®
CORPORATION

7777 W. BLUEMOUND RD. P.O. BOX 13819 MILWAUKEE, WI 53213

Complete songlists and more at **www.halleonard.com**

Prices, contents, and availability subject to change without notice.

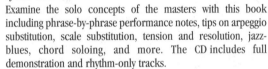